# At the Post Office

Grateful Acknowledgement is made to:
George Bridges, Deborah Hawkins, James Dillliard,
Joan S. Allen, Anthony B. Vaughan, Brian Haywood
Main Post Office, Chicago Illinois

Also to the helpful staff
of the Mankato Post Office, Mankato, MN

**Design and Art Direction**

**Lindaanne Donohoe Design**

**Illustrations**

**Penny Dann**

**Picture Credits**

© Gregg Andersen/Gallery 19: 3, 6, 8, 30
© Phil Martin: cover, 4, 10, 12, 14, 16, 18, 20, 22, 24, 26, 28

●　●　●　●　●　●　●　●　●　●　●　●　●　●

**Library of Congress Cataloging-in-Publication Data**

**Greene, Carol.**

**At the post office / by Carol Greene.**
p.　　cm.
Summary: Takes the readers on a field trip
to a post office where they can walk through
a typical day learning about its functions.
ISBN 1-56766-483-0 (side-sewn  lib. reinforce : alk. paper)
1. Postal service—United States—Juvenile literature.
[1. Postal service.]　I. Title.

HE6371.G74　　1998　　　　　　　　　　　　　97-37748
383'.4973—dc21　　　　　　　　　　　　　　　CIP
　　　　　　　　　　　　　　　　　　　　　　AC

# At the Post Office

## By Carol Greene

### The Child's World®, Inc.

What a big post office!

Trucks bring mail here from smaller post offices.

Mail comes off the truck.

*THUMP! THUMP!*

It moves along on a belt.

This post office helps smaller post offices take care of the mail.

First, people sort the mail.

Letters go one way.

Packages and magazines go another way.

*BUMP! BUMP!*

This woman is sorting through some letters.

Packages come in all sizes.

So do magazines and bundles of ads.

These things are all called "bulk mail."

These packages are very heavy. A worker must pull them around on a flat wagon.

**THUD! THUD!**

Bulk mail will go to a special post office.

Workers take care of all the bulk mail there.

All of this bulk mail is being sent to another post office.

This post office takes care of letters.
*CLICK!  CLICK!*
A machine called an edger-feeder sorts
them all by size. Then it sends the letters
to another machine.

Don't send letters in very small or very large envelopes. The edger-feeder can't sort them.

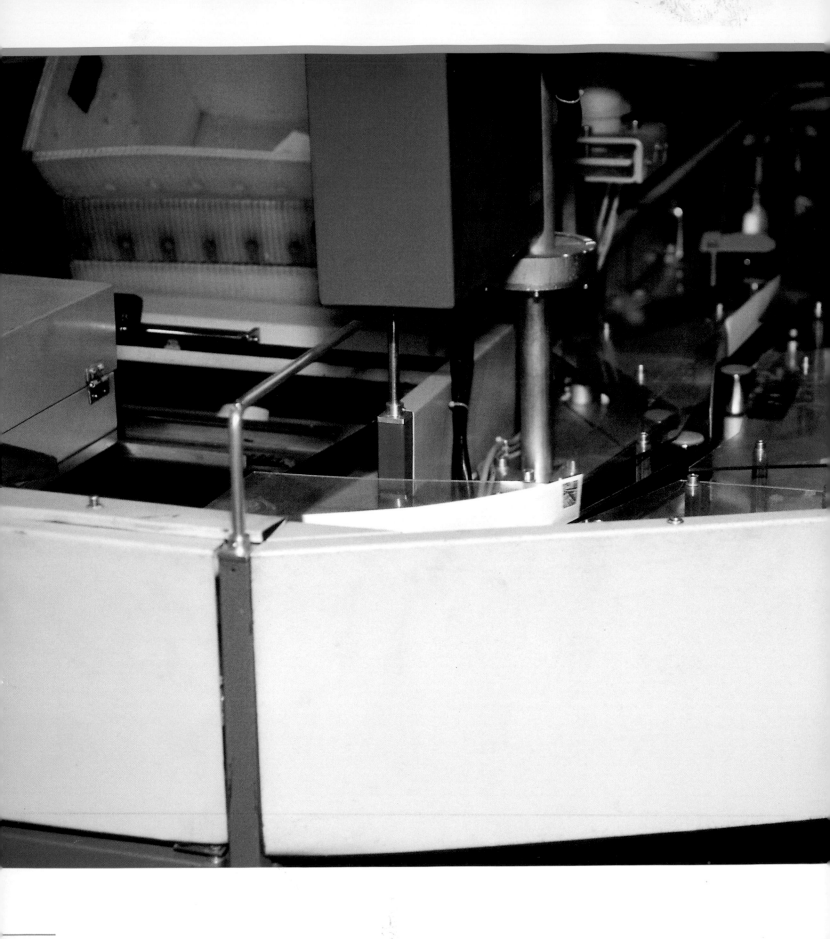

This machine is the facer-canceler.

It makes all the envelopes face the same way.

It prints black lines over the stamps.

Now no one can use the stamps again.

Some facer-cancelers can mark 35,000 letters in an hour.

This worker punches a **ZIP** code into a computer. *ZZZZIP!*

The **ZIP** code tells the machines and the workers where the letter is going.

**THWAP! THWAP! THWAP!**

The letters go into bins.

Each bin holds mail for a different place.

Each place has its own zip code.

ZIP stands for Zone Improvement Plan. ZIP codes make sorting the mail easier.

CLUNK! CLUNK!

The bins full of letters go into these trucks.

*VROOOM! VROOOM!*

Some trucks will carry letters to a post office nearby.

Other trucks will take letters to the airport.

Some letters go across the country.

Some letters go across the world.

**CLANK! FIZZZZZ! EEEEE!**

What a noisy place!

Workers here fix the post office trucks.

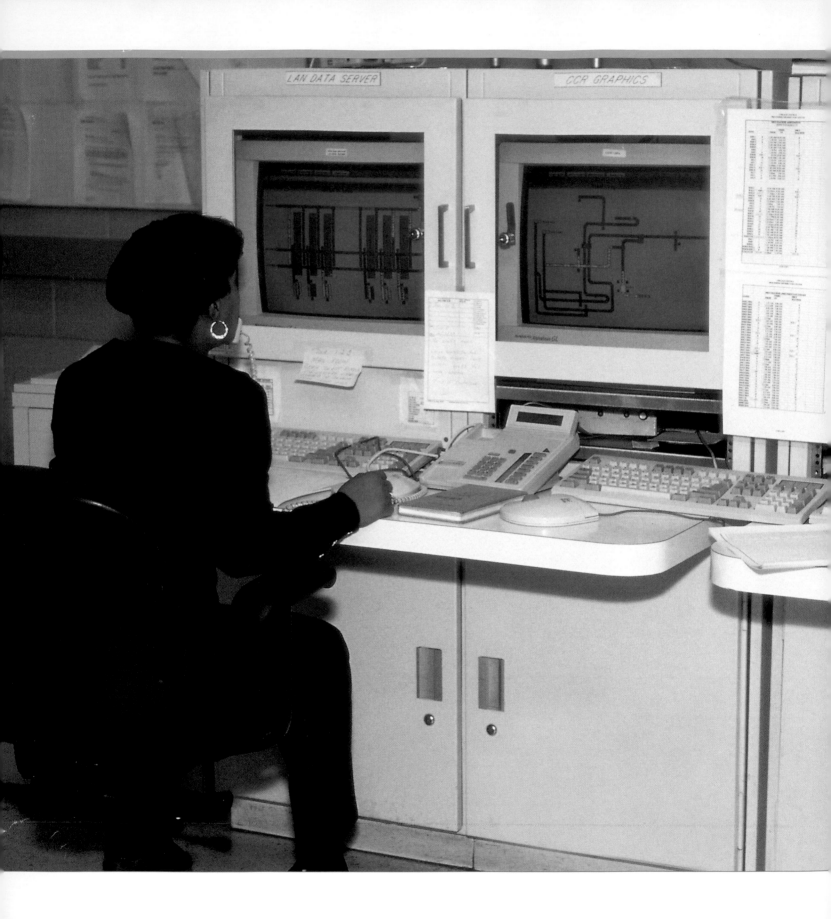

**TAP! TAP! CLICK! CLICK! HUMMM!**

The post office uses many machines.

This control room keeps them running smoothly.

The control room is a little like the post office's brain.

**RRRIP!!**

Sometimes envelopes get torn or break open.
Postal workers fix them. Then they send
the letters on again.

## HMMMMM?

Sometimes no one can read the address on an envelope. Or maybe the sender did not write down the whole address. These letters go to the Dead Letter Office in St. Paul, Minnesota.

The post office in St. Paul keeps dead letters for 90 days. Then it destroys them.

**RUSTLE! CRACKLE!**

You can buy stamps, postcards, and other things here at the post office. Many people buy stamps just to collect them. Every country in the world has its own stamps. Wouldn't you like to see these beautiful and interesting stamps?

Stamp collecting is the most popular hobby in the United States.

## Glossary

**belt** — an endless band that moves things from one place to another

**bin** — a container; box

**bulk mail** — ads and other material sent in large quantities

**control room** — a place equipped to watch over and run all the machines used in an operation

**computer** — a machine built to do mathematical tasks and keep records

**edger-facer** — a machine built to sort envelopes by size

**facer-canceler** — a machine that faces envelopes in the same direction and prints a black mark over stamp

**machine** — a device that does a job

**mail** — letters, magazines, packages, and other objects delivered by postal workers

**ZIP code** — a series of numbers used to identify mail addresses. For example, the first three numbers identify a specific place (often a city), and the next set of numbers tell the postal workers in what part of the city the mail is to be delivered.

**About the Author**
Carol Greene has written over 200 books for children. She also likes to read books, make teddy bears, work in her garden, and sing. Ms. Greene lives in Webster Groves, Missouri.